EMMANUEL JOSEPH

From Steam to Silicon, A Philosophical
History of Technological Revolutions

Contents

Contents

1

Chapter 1: The Dawn of the Industrial Revolution

I n the late 18th century, the world witnessed the birth of the Industrial Revolution, a period that marked a significant shift from agrarian societies to industrialized ones. This transformation was sparked by a series of innovations, most notably the steam engine invented by James Watt. This groundbreaking technology revolutionized industries by providing a reliable and powerful source of energy. Factories began to spring up, and with them came the promise of mass production, increased efficiency, and economic prosperity. The steam engine, powering everything from textile mills to locomotives, symbolized the dawning of a new era of human capability and ambition.

This era was not just about technological advancements; it was also a time of profound philosophical reflection. Thinkers of the time grappled with the implications of mechanization on society and the individual. The shift from manual labor to mechanized production raised questions about the nature of work and the role of humans in the production process. While some celebrated the newfound productivity and wealth, others lamented the loss of traditional skills and the dehumanizing effects of factory life. The philosophical discourse of the period reflected these tensions, as society sought to reconcile the benefits of industrial progress with the costs to human dignity and community.

The impact of the Industrial Revolution extended beyond the factory walls, reshaping entire societies. The rise of industrial cities brought people together in unprecedented numbers, fostering new forms of social organization and interaction. Urbanization, however, also brought challenges such as overcrowding, pollution, and the exploitation of labor. The living conditions in burgeoning industrial towns often starkly contrasted with the utopian visions of progress promised by industrialists. This chapter delves into the realities of life during the early days of the Industrial Revolution, highlighting the complex interplay between technological advancement and social change.

The legacy of the Industrial Revolution is still felt today, as its innovations laid the groundwork for subsequent technological revolutions. The steam engine, in particular, symbolizes the human drive to harness nature's forces for the betterment of society. It serves as a reminder of the transformative power of technology, as well as the need to critically examine the societal impact of each new wave of innovation. By understanding the philosophical and practical implications of this period, we gain valuable insights into the ongoing relationship between technology and humanity.

2

Chapter 2: The Philosophical Roots of Mechanization

Mechanization was not just a technical revolution; it was also a profound philosophical shift. The introduction of machines into the production process brought about new ways of thinking about labor, efficiency, and the role of humans in industry. Key thinkers of the time, such as Adam Smith and Karl Marx, provided contrasting views on these changes. Smith, often regarded as the father of modern economics, saw mechanization as a path to greater productivity and economic prosperity. He argued that the division of labor, enabled by machines, would lead to increased efficiency and wealth.

In contrast, Karl Marx offered a more critical perspective on mechanization. He warned of the dehumanizing effects of industrial capitalism and the alienation of workers from the products of their labor. According to Marx, machines reduced workers to mere cogs in a vast industrial machine, stripping them of their individuality and creativity. This chapter delves into the philosophical debates between proponents of mechanization and its critics, highlighting the tensions between economic progress and human dignity.

The philosophical roots of mechanization also extended to broader ethical questions about the nature of work and the value of human labor. As machines took over tasks previously performed by humans, questions arose about the purpose and meaning of work. Was labor merely a means to an end, or did it hold intrinsic value? These debates were not merely academic; they had real-world implications for the organization of society and the treatment of workers. The Industrial Revolution forced society to confront these questions in new and urgent ways.

Ultimately, the philosophical roots of mechanization laid the foundation for modern industrial society. The ideas and debates of this period continue to influence contemporary discussions about technology, labor, and ethics. By examining the philosophical underpinnings of mechanization, we can better understand the ongoing relationship between humans and machines and the complex interplay between technology and society.

3

Chapter 3: The Rise of the Factory System

The factory system brought about profound changes in the way people lived and worked. Prior to the Industrial Revolution, most production took place in small workshops or homes. The advent of factories centralized production, leading to the growth of urban centers and the rise of a new industrial working class. Factories enabled the mass production of goods, increasing efficiency and lowering costs. However, this shift also brought challenges, including harsh working conditions, long hours, and the exploitation of labor.

The factory system raised significant ethical and philosophical questions. The concentration of workers in factories created new forms of social stratification and inequality. Factory owners amassed significant wealth, while workers often toiled in dangerous and unhealthy conditions for meager wages. This disparity led to debates about the responsibilities of industrialists and the rights of workers. The rise of the labor movement and the push for workers' rights were direct responses to the inequalities of the factory system.

The factory system also had a profound impact on the daily lives of workers. The rigid schedules and repetitive tasks of factory work contrasted sharply with the more flexible and varied rhythms of pre-industrial labor. This shift raised questions about the nature of work and its impact on human well-being. Critics argued that the factory system dehumanized workers, reducing them to mere instruments of production. Supporters, on the other hand, saw it as a means of achieving economic progress and improving standards of living.

Despite its challenges, the factory system played a crucial role in the development of modern industrial society. It enabled the production of goods on a scale previously unimaginable, contributing to economic growth and the rise of consumer culture. The ethical and philosophical questions raised by the factory system continue to resonate today, as we grapple with the impact of technology and industrialization on labor, society, and human dignity.

4

Chapter 4: The Spread of Industrialization Globally

I ndustrialization did not remain confined to Europe; it spread to other parts of the world, transforming economies and societies. Countries like the United States, Japan, and Russia embraced industrialization, each with their own unique challenges and adaptations. In the United States, the expansion of the railroads and the rise of factories transformed the nation into an economic powerhouse. Industrialization brought about significant social changes, including urbanization and the rise of a new middle class.

In Japan, the Meiji Restoration marked a period of rapid industrialization and modernization. The Japanese government actively promoted industrial development, investing in infrastructure and adopting Western technologies. This transformation enabled Japan to become a major industrial and military power. However, industrialization also brought about social upheaval and tensions between traditional and modern values.

Russia's industrialization was marked by a different trajectory. The country lagged behind Western Europe in industrial development, but the late 19th and early 20th centuries saw significant efforts to catch up. The Russian government implemented policies to promote industrialization, including the construction of railroads and the establishment of factories. However, the rapid pace of change also contributed to social unrest and played a role in the eventual Russian Revolution.

The global spread of industrialization had profound philosophical implications. Different cultures grappled with the challenges and opportunities of industrialization in unique ways, leading to diverse responses and adaptations. The diffusion of industrial technology also raised questions about cultural exchange, imperialism, and the impact of globalization. This chapter explores the global dimensions of industrialization and the philosophical questions it raised in different contexts.

5

Chapter 5: The Advent of Electricity

The discovery and harnessing of electricity marked a new era in technological advancement. Innovators like Thomas Edison and Nikola Tesla revolutionized the way we live and work by tapping into the power of electricity. Edison, with his invention of the practical incandescent light bulb, brought light to homes and factories, extending working hours and improving the quality of life. Tesla's contributions to the development of alternating current (AC) technology enabled the efficient transmission of electricity over long distances, making it accessible to a wider population.

The advent of electricity had profound philosophical implications. It transformed the rhythm of daily life, allowing activities to continue long after sunset. The ability to illuminate the night challenged the natural order and extended human control over the environment. This newfound power raised questions about the relationship between humans and nature, and the ethical responsibilities that come with such control. The electrification of homes and cities also brought about new forms of social interaction and community, as people gathered in newly lit public spaces.

The impact of electricity extended beyond lighting. It powered factories, enabling the use of electric machinery and increasing industrial productivity. This shift had significant implications for labor, as workers adapted to new technologies and production methods. The rise of electric-powered factories also contributed to urbanization, as people moved to cities in search of employment. The centralization of power generation and distribution raised ethical questions about access, equity, and the environmental impact of electricity production.

Electricity's role in communication and entertainment further transformed society. The invention of the telegraph and telephone facilitated instant communication across long distances, shrinking the world and connecting people in new ways. The development of radio and later television brought information and entertainment into homes, shaping public discourse and cultural norms. This chapter delves into the philosophical impact of electrification on society, exploring the ways in which electricity reshaped human experiences and relationships.

6

Chapter 6: The Birth of Telecommunications

T elecommunications bridged vast distances, allowing for instant communication across continents. The invention of the telegraph in the 19th century was a game-changer, enabling messages to be sent and received in real-time. This innovation revolutionized industries such as journalism, commerce, and diplomacy, as information could be transmitted quickly and efficiently. The telephone, invented by Alexander Graham Bell, further transformed communication by allowing people to speak directly to one another across long distances.

The birth of telecommunications raised significant ethical and philosophical questions. The ability to communicate instantaneously challenged traditional notions of time and space, collapsing geographical barriers and creating a more interconnected world. This newfound connectivity had both positive and negative implications. On one hand, it facilitated global cooperation and the exchange of ideas. On the other hand, it also raised concerns about privacy, surveillance, and the potential for information overload.

The impact of telecommunications extended to the social fabric of society. The ability to communicate across distances changed the nature of relationships, as people could maintain connections with friends and family members far away. However, it also raised questions about the quality of these interactions and the potential for virtual communication to replace face-to-face contact. The rise of telecommunications also contributed to the growth of new forms of media, such as radio and television, which played a significant role in shaping public opinion and cultural norms.

The philosophical implications of telecommunications continue to resonate in the digital age. The development of the internet and mobile technologies has further transformed communication, raising new ethical questions about data privacy, digital rights, and the impact of technology on human relationships. By examining the birth of telecommunications and its philosophical impact, we gain insights into the ongoing evolution of communication technologies and their role in shaping society.

7

Chapter 7: The Rise of Automobiles

The automobile revolutionized transportation, making travel faster and more accessible. Henry Ford's introduction of the assembly line in the early 20th century brought cars to the masses, significantly lowering the cost of production and making automobiles affordable for many people. This innovation not only transformed the automotive industry but also had a profound impact on society as a whole.

The rise of automobiles raised important philosophical and ethical questions. The increased mobility afforded by cars changed the way people lived and worked, enabling suburbanization and the growth of new communities. However, it also contributed to urban sprawl, environmental pollution, and a dependence on fossil fuels. These issues prompted debates about the sustainability of the automobile-centric lifestyle and the need for alternative modes of transportation.

The automobile also had a significant impact on individual freedom and autonomy. The ability to travel independently gave people greater control over their movements and expanded their horizons. However, it also raised questions about the societal costs of this newfound freedom, including traffic congestion, road accidents, and the impact on public health. The philosophical implications of the automobile extend to debates about the balance between individual rights and collective responsibilities in the context of transportation.

The cultural impact of the automobile cannot be overstated. Cars became symbols of status, identity, and personal expression, shaping popular culture and influencing social norms. The rise of car culture also brought about new forms of entertainment, such as road trips and drive-in theaters, further embedding the automobile in the fabric of society. This chapter explores the philosophical and ethical questions raised by the rise of automobiles, examining their impact on individual freedom, urban planning, and environmental sustainability.

8

Chapter 8: The Age of Aviation

The invention of the airplane opened up the skies, shrinking the world and making international travel possible. Pioneers like the Wright brothers and Amelia Earhart pushed the boundaries of human achievement, demonstrating the potential of flight to connect people and cultures. The age of aviation transformed transportation, enabling rapid movement across vast distances and facilitating global trade and communication.

The philosophical significance of aviation extends beyond the practical benefits of air travel. The ability to soar above the earth offered new perspectives on the world, challenging traditional notions of distance, time, and space. Aviation also raised ethical questions about the impact of air travel on the environment, including issues of carbon emissions and the sustainability of the aviation industry. These concerns prompted debates about the responsibility of individuals and governments in addressing the environmental impact of air travel.

Aviation also had a profound impact on global connectivity and cultural exchange. The ease of international travel facilitated the spread of ideas, technologies, and cultural practices, contributing to the process of globalization. However, it also raised questions about cultural homogenization and the potential loss of local identities. The philosophical implications of aviation extend to debates about the balance between the benefits of global connectivity and the preservation of cultural diversity.

The age of aviation also brought about new forms of innovation and exploration. The development of commercial airlines made air travel accessible to a broader population, while advances in aerospace technology enabled the exploration of space. This chapter explores the philosophical questions raised by the age of aviation, examining its impact on globalization, cultural exchange, and the perception of distance and time.

9

Chapter 9: The Space Age

T he space race of the mid-20th century marked humanity's quest to explore beyond our planet. The competition between the United States and the Soviet Union to achieve spaceflight milestones captured the world's imagination and demonstrated the potential of human ingenuity. The successful launch of Sputnik by the Soviet Union in 1957 and the subsequent moon landing by NASA's Apollo 11 mission in 1969 were monumental achievements that expanded our horizons and challenged our understanding of the universe.

The Space Age had profound philosophical implications. It prompted humanity to contemplate our place in the cosmos and the possibilities of space exploration. The images of Earth from space, such as the iconic "Blue Marble" photograph, fostered a sense of global unity and environmental awareness. This new perspective raised ethical questions about our responsibilities to the planet and the potential impact of space exploration on Earth's ecosystems.

Space exploration also spurred debates about the search for extraterrestrial life and the ethical considerations of space colonization. The possibility of encountering other intelligent beings challenged our understanding of life and consciousness, prompting questions about the nature of existence and our place in the universe. The ethical implications of space colonization included concerns about the potential exploitation of extraterrestrial resources and the need to ensure that space exploration benefits all of humanity.

The Space Age also brought about new technological advancements and innovations. The development of space travel technologies, such as rockets and satellites, had far-reaching applications beyond space exploration. These technologies contributed to advancements in communication, weather forecasting, and scientific research. This chapter examines the philosophical questions raised by the Space Age, exploring the impact of space exploration on our understanding of the universe and our responsibilities as stewards of Earth and beyond.

10

Chapter 10: The Digital Revolution

The advent of computers and the digital age transformed every aspect of our lives. From the early days of mainframes to the rise of personal computers and the internet, the digital revolution brought about unprecedented changes in how we work, communicate, and access information. This chapter traces the evolution of digital technology and its impact on society.

The digital revolution had significant philosophical implications. The development of artificial intelligence (AI) and machine learning raised questions about the nature of intelligence and consciousness. The possibility of creating machines that could think and learn challenged traditional notions of what it means to be human. These developments prompted ethical debates about the responsibilities of AI developers and the potential consequences of creating intelligent machines.

The digital age also brought about new forms of communication and information sharing. The internet connected people across the globe, creating a vast network of knowledge and resources. However, this newfound connectivity also raised concerns about data privacy, digital rights, and the impact of technology on human relationships. The rise of social media platforms further transformed communication, raising questions about the quality of online interactions and the potential for misinformation.

The digital revolution also had a profound impact on the nature of work.

Automation and digital technologies reshaped industries, leading to changes in employment patterns and the skills required in the workforce. This shift raised ethical questions about the future of work and the need to ensure that technological advancements benefit all members of society. This chapter explores the philosophical implications of the digital revolution, examining the ways in which digital technologies have reshaped our lives and the ethical considerations they raise.

11

Chapter 11: The Rise of Silicon Valley

S ilicon Valley became the epicenter of technological innovation, producing companies and technologies that shaped the digital age. This region in Northern California attracted some of the brightest minds and boldest entrepreneurs, leading to the creation of groundbreaking technologies and iconic companies. The culture of innovation in Silicon Valley was characterized by a willingness to take risks, challenge established norms, and disrupt traditional industries.

The rise of Silicon Valley raised important philosophical and ethical questions. The rapid pace of technological advancement prompted debates about the ethics of disruption and the impact of innovation on society. While some celebrated the transformative potential of new technologies, others raised concerns about the consequences of disruption for workers, industries, and communities. The culture of Silicon Valley also raised questions about the values that underpin technological innovation and the responsibilities of tech companies.

Silicon Valley's influence extended beyond technology to broader societal and cultural trends. The region's emphasis on entrepreneurship and innovation inspired similar ecosystems around the world, contributing to the globalization of the tech industry. However, it also raised questions about the concentration of power and wealth in the hands of a few tech giants. The dominance of companies like Google, Apple, and Facebook prompted debates about corporate responsibility, antitrust regulations, and the ethical implications of technological monopolies.

The rise of Silicon Valley also highlighted the importance of diversity and inclusion in the tech industry. The lack of representation of women and minorities in tech companies raised questions about equality and access to opportunities. Efforts to address these issues included initiatives to promote diversity and inclusion, as well as broader discussions about the role of technology in shaping social and economic inequalities. This chapter explores the philosophical questions raised by the rise of Silicon Valley, examining the impact of innovation on society and the ethical considerations of technological advancement.

12

Chapter 12: The Internet and Global Connectivity

The internet revolutionized the way we access information and communicate. It created a global village, bringing people closer together while also raising concerns about digital divides and information overload. This chapter examines the ethical and philosophical implications of the internet, including issues of censorship, digital rights, and the democratization of information.

The internet's impact on information access and sharing was profound. It provided a platform for the free flow of information, enabling people to access knowledge and resources from around the world. However, this newfound openness also raised concerns about the quality and reliability of online information. The spread of misinformation and fake news prompted debates about the responsibilities of online platforms and the need for digital literacy.

The internet also transformed the nature of communication and social interaction. Social media platforms and messaging apps enabled people to connect and share with others across the globe. However, these new forms of communication also raised questions about privacy, data security, and the impact of digital interactions on mental health. The internet's role in shaping public discourse and influencing political processes further highlighted the need for ethical considerations in online communication.

The internet's potential for democratizing information and empowering individuals was significant. It provided a platform for marginalized voices and facilitated grassroots movements and social activism. However, it also raised questions about access and equity, as digital divides persisted, limiting the benefits of the internet to certain populations. Efforts to address these issues included initiatives to expand internet access and promote digital inclusion.

The philosophical implications of the internet extend to debates about the nature of information, knowledge, and communication in the digital age. The internet's impact on society and culture continues to evolve, raising new ethical questions and challenges. This chapter explores the philosophical questions raised by the internet, examining its role in shaping global connectivity and the ethical considerations of the digital age.

13

Chapter 13: The Rise of Social Media

S ocial media platforms transformed how we interact, share, and consume content. The rise of platforms such as Facebook, Twitter, and Instagram created new forms of community and self-expression. These platforms enabled people to connect with friends and family, share their experiences, and engage with a global audience. However, the rise of social media also brought about new challenges and ethical questions.

The impact of social media on identity and relationships was profound. The ability to curate and share personal content enabled people to present themselves in new ways, shaping their online identities. This shift raised questions about the authenticity of online personas and the potential for social media to create unrealistic expectations and pressures. The nature of relationships also changed, as social media facilitated connections with a broader network of people while raising concerns about the quality and depth of these interactions.

Social media also had significant implications for public discourse and the spread of information. The platforms provided a space for diverse voices and opinions, enabling new forms of activism and social engagement. However, they also contributed to the spread of misinformation and the polarization of public opinion. The algorithms that governed content visibility raised ethical questions about the responsibility of social media companies in shaping public discourse and the potential for echo chambers and filter bubbles.

The rise of social media brought about new concerns regarding privacy and data security. The collection and use of personal data by social media companies raised questions about the ownership and control of digital information. High-profile data breaches and scandals, such as the Cambridge Analytica incident, highlighted the need for greater transparency and accountability in data practices. This chapter explores the philosophical and ethical questions raised by the rise of social media, examining its impact on identity, relationships, and public discourse.

14

Chapter 14: The Future of Artificial Intelligence

rtificial intelligence promises to revolutionize industries and
reshape society in profound ways. The development of AI
technologies, such as machine learning and neural networks, has
enabled machines to perform tasks that were once the exclusive domain of
humans. From self-driving cars to natural language processing, AI has the
potential to transform various aspects of our lives.

The philosophical questions raised by AI are numerous and complex. One
of the central debates concerns the nature of intelligence and consciousness.
Can machines truly be intelligent, or are they simply following programmed
instructions? The possibility of creating conscious machines raises questions
about the nature of personhood and the ethical treatment of AI entities. These
debates challenge our understanding of what it means to be human and the
boundaries between humans and machines.

AI also raises significant ethical considerations regarding its development
and deployment. The use of AI in decision-making processes, such as hiring or
sentencing, has the potential to introduce biases and perpetuate inequalities.
Ensuring fairness and transparency in AI systems is a critical concern, as is the
need to address the potential for job displacement and economic disruption.
The development of ethical guidelines and regulations for AI is an ongoing

and essential task.

The future of AI also prompts questions about the relationship between humans and technology. As AI becomes more integrated into our daily lives, we must consider the impact on human autonomy and creativity. Will AI enhance our capabilities, or will it undermine our sense of agency and purpose? This chapter explores the philosophical and ethical implications of AI, examining the potential benefits and challenges of this transformative technology.

15

Chapter 15: The Ethical Implications of Technological Revolutions

As we look to the future, it is essential to consider the ethical implications of technological advancements. Each technological revolution, from steam to silicon, has brought about significant changes in society and raised important ethical questions. The lessons learned from past technological revolutions can inform our approach to future innovations, ensuring that technology serves the greater good.

The ethical implications of technological revolutions extend to various aspects of society, including labor, environment, and equity. Technological advancements have the potential to improve living standards and create new opportunities, but they also pose risks such as job displacement, environmental degradation, and social inequalities. Addressing these challenges requires a commitment to responsible innovation and ethical considerations in the development and deployment of new technologies.

The role of ethics in technological innovation is particularly important as we navigate the complexities of the digital age. Issues such as data privacy, digital rights, and the impact of AI on society require careful consideration and regulation. Ensuring that technological advancements align with ethical principles and societal values is a collective responsibility that involves policymakers, technologists, and the broader public.

The philosophical questions raised by technological revolutions also prompt us to reflect on our values and aspirations as a society. What kind of future do we want to create, and how can technology help us achieve it? By examining the ethical implications of technological advancements, we can better navigate the challenges and opportunities of the future. This chapter calls for a balance between progress and ethical considerations, emphasizing the importance of responsible innovation in shaping a better world.

Book Description:

In **"From Steam to Silicon: A Philosophical History of Technological Revolutions,"** embark on a journey through the transformative epochs that have shaped our modern world. This compelling exploration delves into the heart of technological advancements, from the steam engines of the Industrial Revolution to the silicon chips driving today's digital age.

Each chapter unveils the stories of visionary inventors and the groundbreaking innovations that redefined societies, economies, and human experiences. Beyond the technical marvels, this book probes the profound philosophical questions these revolutions have raised. It examines the ethical dilemmas, societal impacts, and the eternal quest for progress that accompany each technological leap.

From the rise of factories and the dawn of electricity to the advent of telecommunications, automobiles, aviation, and the space age, the narrative threads the philosophical underpinnings that have influenced thinkers and leaders. It takes readers through the digital revolution, the cultural phenomenon of Silicon Valley, and the pervasive connectivity of the internet, culminating in the ethical considerations of artificial intelligence and the future of technological innovations.

"From Steam to Silicon" offers a thoughtful reflection on how technology shapes our lives and values. It serves as a reminder that while technology propels us forward, it also compels us to confront the ethical and philosophical dimensions of our progress. This book is a must-read for anyone curious about the intertwined history of technology and philosophy and the path that has led us to our present and future.

www.ingramcontent.com/pod-product-compliance
Lightning Source LLC
Chambersburg PA
CBHW070928050326
40689CB00015B/3662